CRITTERS
CRIATURAS DE LA NATURALEZA

Grow a bilingual vocabulary by:

- **Looking** at pictures and words
- **Talking** about what you see
- **Touching** and naming objects
- **Using** questions to extend learning...
  Ask questions that invite children
  to share information.
  Begin your questions with words like...
  who, what, when, where and how.

Aumenta tu vocabulario bilingüe:

- **Mirando** las imágenes y las palabras
- **Hablando** de lo que ves
- **Tocando** y nombrando los objetos
- **Usando** preguntas para aumentar el aprendizaje...
  Usa preguntas que inviten a los niños a compartir
  la información.
  Empieza tus frases con el uso de estas palabras:
  ¿quién? ¿qué? ¿cuándo? ¿dónde? y ¿cómo?

These books support a series of educational games by Learning Props.
Estos libros refuerzan una serie de juegos educativos desarrollados por Learning Props.
Learning Props, L.L.C., P.O. Box 774, Racine, WI 53401-0774
1-877-776-7750   www.learningprops.com

Created by/Creado por: Bev Schumacher, Learning Props, L.L.C.
Graphic Design/Diseñadora gráfica: Bev Kirk
Images/Fotos: Photos.com, 123rf.com, Hemera Technologies Inc., Dawn Lund, Laura Schumacher
Spanish Translation/Traducción al español: Myriam Sosa, Rosana Sartirana
Thanks to the Racine Zoological Society Conservation Education Department for technical support.
Gracias al Racine Zoological Society Conservation Education Department por el soporte técnico.

Library of Congress Control Number 2008907373   ISBN 978-1-935292-04-3

 # On the farm...
En la granja...

dairy cow
la vaca lechera

beef cow
la vaca para carne

sheep
la oveja

donkey
el burro

duck
el pato

turkey
el pavo/
el guajolote

horse
el caballo

goat
la cabra

llama
la llama

chickens
las gallinas/los pollos

rooster
el gallo

hen
la gallina

pigs
los cerdos/
los cochinos

At the zoo...
En el zoológico...

zebras
las cebras

panda
el oso panda

buffalo
el búfalo

peacock
el pavo real

camels
los camellos

kangaroo
el canguro

orangutan
el orangután

chimpanzees
los chimpancés

ostrich
el avestruz

koala
el koala

elephant
el elefante

giraffe
la jirafa

 # In the air...
En el aire...

seagull
la gaviota

fly
la mosca

dragonfly
la libélula

bat
el murciélago

butterfly
la mariposa

robin
el tordo/
el petirrojo

bee
la abeja

eagle
el águila

sparrow
el gorrión

owl
el búho/la lechuza

pigeons
las palomas

 # In the forest...
En el bosque...

bear
el oso

deer
el ciervo/el venado

earthworm
la lombriz
de tierra

rabbit
el conejo

grasshopper
el saltamontes

fox
el zorro

spider
la araña

caterpillar
la oruga/
el gusano

squirrel
la ardilla

ladybug
la mariquita/
la vaquita
de San Antonio

chipmunk
la ardilla

skunk
la mofeta/el zorrillo/
el zorrino

snake
la culebra/la serpiente/
la víbora

In the water...
En el agua...

dolphins
los delfines

starfish
la estrella de mar

shark
el tiburón

sea horse
el caballito de mar

lobster
la langosta

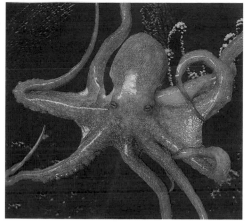

octopus
el pulpo

clownfish
el pez payaso

seal
la foca

whale
la ballena

goldfish
los pecesitos dorados

 # Near the water...
Cerca del agua...

swan
el cisne

alligator
el lagarto/
el caimán

frog
la rana

polar bears
los osos polares

goose
el ganso

tortoise
la tortuga

raccoon
el mapache

duck
el pato

flamingo
el flamenco/
el flamingo

snail
el caracol

penguins
los pingüinos

 # In the jungle...
En la selva...

monkey
el mono/el chango

elephants
los elefantes

gorilla
el gorila

chameleon
el camaleón

tigers
los tigres

In the grasslands...
En las praderas...

cheetah
la onza/la chita

rhinoceros
el rinoceronte

baboons
los monos
babuinos

giraffe
la jirafa

lion
el león

Baby animals...
La cría de los animales...

bear & cubs
el oso y sus
cachorros

kangaroo & joey

el canguro y
el cangurito

zebra & colt
la cebra y
el padrillo

cow & calf
la vaca y
el becerro

cat & kitten
el gato y el gatito

leopard & cub
el leopardo y
su cachorro

duck & ducklings
el pato y
los patitos

elephant & calf
el elefante y su cría

lion & cubs
el león y sus cachorros

orangutan & baby
el orangután y su cría

horse & colt
el caballo y el potrillo

monkey & baby
el mono y su cría

pig & piglets
**el cochino y
los cochinillos**

dog & puppy
**el perro y
su cachorro**

Pets...
Las mascotas...

goldfish
los pecesitos dorados

parakeet
el periquito/ la cotorra

dog
el perro

turtle
la tortuga

guinea pig
el cobaya/el cochinito de guinea

rabbit
el conejo

cat
el gato

pronunciation la pronunciación

Critters/**Krit**-urs *Criaturas De La Naturaleza*/Kree-ah-**too**-rahs Day Lah Nah-too-rah-**lay**-sah
on the farm/**on** THuh **farm** en la granja/ayn lah **grahn**-hah
at the zoo/**at** THuh **zoo** en el zoológico/ayn ayl soh-**loh**-hee-koh
in the air/**in** THuh **air** en el aire/ayn ayl **ah**-ee-ray
in the forest/**in** THuh **for**-ist en el bosque/ayn ayl **bohs**-kay
in the water/**in** THuh **waw**-tur en el agua/ayn ayl **ah**-goo-ah
near the water/**nihr** THuh **waw**-tur cerca del agua/**sayr**-kah dayl **ah**-goo-ah
in the jungle/**in** THuh **juhng**-guhl en la selva/ayn lah **sayl**-vah
in the grasslands/**in** THuh **grass**-lands en las praderas/ayn lahs prah-**day**-rahs
baby animals/**bay**-bee **an**-uh-muhlss la cría de los animales/lah **kree**-ah day lohs ah-nee-**mah**-lays
pets/**petss** las mascotas/lahs mahs-**koh**-tahs

alligator/**al**-i-gay-tuhr el lagarto, el caimán/
ayl lah-**gahr**-toh, ayl kah-ee-**mahn**
baboon(s)/ba-**boon(ss)** los monos babuinos/
lohs **moh**-nohs bah-boo-**ee**-nohs
baby/**bay**-bee su cría/soo **kree**-ah
bat/**bat** el murciélago/ayl moor-see-**ay**-lah-goh
bear/**bair** el oso/ayl **oh**-soh
bee/**bee** la abeja/lah ah-**bay**-ha
beef cow/**beef kou** la vaca para carne/
lah **vah**-kah **pah**-rah **kahr**-nay
buffalo / **buhf**-uh-loh el búfalo/ayl **boo**-fah-loh
butterfly/**buht**-ur-flye la mariposa/
lah mah-ree-**poh**-sah
calf/**kaf** el becerro/ayl bay-**say** rroh
camel(s)/**kam**-uhl(ss) los camellos/
lohs kah-**may**-yohs
cat/**kat** el gato/ayl **gah**-toh
caterpillar/**kat**-ur-pil-ur la oruga, el gusano/
lah oh-**roo**-gah, ayl goo-**sah**-noh
chameleon/kuh-**mee**-lee-uhn el camaleón/
ayl kah-mah-lay-**ohn**
cheetah/**chee**-tuh la onza, la chita/lah **ohn**-sah,
lah **shee**-tah
chicken(s)/**chick**-uhn(ss) las gallinas, los pollos/
lahs gah-**yee**-nahs, lohs **poh**-yohs
chimpanzee(s)/chim-**pan**-zee(ss)
los chimpancés/lohs sheem-pahn-**says**
chipmunk/**chip**-muhnk la ardilla/lah ahr-**dee**-yah

clownfish/**kloun**-fish el pez payaso/
ayl pays pah-**yah**-soh
colt/**kohlt** el padrillo/ayl pah-**dree**-yoh
el potrillo/ayl **poh**-tree-**yoh**
cow/**kou** la vaca/lah **vah**-kah
cub(s)/**kuhb(z)** su cachorro/soo kah-**shoh**-rroh,
sus cachorros/soos kah-**shoh**-rrohs
dairy cow/**dair**-ee **kou** la vaca lechera/
lah **vah**-kah lay-**shay**-rah
deer/**dihr** el ciervo, el venado/ayl see-**ayr**-voh,
ayl vay-**nah**-doh
dog/**dawg** el perro/ayl **pay**-rroh
dolphin(s)/**dol**-fin(ss) los delfines/
lohs dayl-**fee**-nays
donkey/**dong**-kee el burro/ayl **boo**-rroh
dragonfly/**drag**-uhn-flye la libélula/
lah lee-**bay**-loo-lah
duck/**duhk** el pato/ayl **pah**-toh
duckling(s)/**duhk**-ling(z) los patitos/
lohs pah-**tee**-tohs
eagle/**ee**-guhl el águila/ayl **ah**-gee-lah
earthworm/**urth**-wurm la lombriz de tierra/
lah lohm-**brees** day tee-**ay**-rrah
elephant(s)/**el**-uh-fuhnt(ss) el elefante/ayl
ay-lay-**fahn**-tay, los elefantes/lohs ay-lay-**fahn**-tays
flamingo/fluh-**ming**-goh el flamenco, el flamingo/
ayl flah-**mayn**-koh, ayl flah-**meen**-goh
fly/**flye** la mosca/lah **mohs**-kah

fox/**foks** el zorro/ayl **soh**-rroh
frog/**frawg** la rana/lah **rrah**-nah
giraffe/juh-**raf** la jirafa/lah hee-**rah**-fah
goat/**goht** la cabra/lah **kah**-brah
goldfish/**gohld**-fish los pecesitos dorados/
lohs pay-say-**see**-tohs doh-**rah**-dohs
goose/**gooss** el ganso/ayl **gahn**-soh
gorilla/guh-**ril**-uh el gorila/ayl goh-**ree**-lah
grasshopper/**grass**-hop-ur el saltamontes/
ayl sahl-tah-**mohn**-tays
guinea pig/**gin**-ee **pig** el cobaya, el cochinito de
guinea/ayl koh-**bah**-yah, ayl koh-shee-**nee**-toh
day gee-**nay**-ah
hen/**hen** la gallina/lah gah-**yee**-nah
horse/**horss** el caballo/ayl kah-**bah**-yoh
joey/**jo**-ee el cangurito/ayl kahn-goo-**ree**-toh
kangaroo/kang-guh-**roo** el canguro/
ayl kahn-**goo**-roh
kitten/**kit**-uhn el gatito/ayl gah-**tee**-toh
koala/**koh**-ah-luh el koala/ayl koh-**ah**-lah
ladybug/**lay**-dee-buhg la mariquita, la vaquita de
San Antonio/lah mah-ree-**kee**-tah,
lah vah-**kee**-tah day Sahn Ahn-**toh**-nee-oh
leopard/**lep**-urd el leopardo/ayl lay-oh-**pahr**-doh
lion/**lye**-uhn el león/ayl lay-**ohn**
llama/**lah**-muh la llama/lah **yah**-mah
lobster/**lob**-stur la langosta/lah lahn-**gohs**-tah
monkey/**muhng**-kee el mono, el chango/
ayl **moh**-noh, ayl **shahn**-goh
octopus/**ok**-tuh-puhss el pulpo/ayl **pool**-poh
orangutan/uh-**rang**-uh-tan el orangután/
ayl oh-rahn-goo-**tahn**
ostrich/**oss**-trich el avestruz/ayl ah-vays-**troos**
owl/**oul** el búho, la lechuza/ayl **boo**-oh,
lah lay-**shoo**-sah
panda/**pan**-duh el oso panda/
ayl **oh**-soh **pahn**-dah
parakeet/**pa**-ruh-keet el periquito, la cotorra/
ayl pay-ree-**kee**-toh, lah koh-**toh**-rrah
peacock/**pee**-kok el pavo real/ayl **pah**-voh
rray-**ahl**
penguin(s)/**peng**-gwin(ss) los pingüinos/
lohs peen-goo-**ee**-nohs

pig(s)/**pig(z)** el cochino/ayl koh-**shee**-noh,
los cerdos, los cochinos/
lohs **sayr**-dohs, lohs koh-**shee**-nohs
pigeon(s)/**pij**-uhn(z) las palomas/
lahs pah-**loh**-mahs
piglet(s)/**pig**-let(ss) los cochinillos/
lohs koh-shee-**nee**-yohs
polar bear(s)/**poh**-lur **bair(z)** los osos polares/
lohs **oh**-sohs poh-**lah**-rays
puppy/**puhp**-ee su cachorro/soo kah-shoh-**rroh**
rabbit/**rab**-it el conejo/ayl koh-**nay**-hoh
raccoon/ra-**koon** el mapache/ayl mah-**pah**-shay
rhinoceros/rye-**noss**-ur-uhss el rinoceronte/
ayl rree-noh-say-**rohn**-tay
robin/**rob**-in el tordo, el petirrojo/ayl **tohr**-doh,
ayl pay-tee-**rroh**-ho
rooster/**roo**-stur el gallo/ayl **gah**-yoh
sea horse/**see horss** el caballito de mar/
ayl kah-bah-**yee**-toh day mahr
seagull/**see**-guhl la gaviota/lah gah-vee-**oh**-tah
seal/**seel** la foca/lah **foh**-kah
shark/**shark** el tiburón/ayl tee-boo-**rohn**
sheep/**sheep** la oveja/lah oh-**vay**-hah
skunk/**skuhngk** la mofeta, el zorrillo, el zorrino/
lah moh-**fay**-tah, ayl soh-**rree**-yoh,
ayl soh-**rree**-noh
snail/**snayl** el caracol/ayl kah-rah-**kohl**
snake/**snayk** la culebra, la serpiente, la víbora/
lah koo-**lay**-brah, lah sayr-pee-**ayn**-tay,
lah **vee**-boh-rah
sparrow/**spa**-roh el gorrión/ayl goh-rree-**ohn**
spider/**spye**-dur la araña/lah ah-**rah**-nyah
squirrel/**skwurl** la ardilla/lah ahr-**dee**-yah
starfish/**star**-fish la estrella de mar/
lah ays-**tray**-yah day mahr
swan/**swahn** el cisne/ayl **sees**-nay
tiger(s)/**tye**-gur(z) los tigres/lohs **tee**-grays
tortoise/**tor**-tuhss la tortuga/lah tohr-**too**-gah
turkey/**tur**-kee el pavo, el guajolote/ayl **pah**-voh,
ayl goo-ah-ho-**loh**-tay
turtle/**tur**-tuhl la tortuga/lah tohr-**too**-gah
whale/**wale** la ballena/lah bah-**yay**-nah
zebra(s)/**zee**-bruh(z) la cebra/lah **say**-brah,
las cebras/lahs **say**-brahs